Our Mother,
The Mountain

Abunden Shalem Joseph

So nice to meet
A new
Generation
of
Mountain
Kids

Our Mother, The Mountain
© Alexander Shalom Joseph, 2022

Books may be purchased in quantity and/or special sales by
contacting the publisher. All inquiries related to such
matters should be addressed to:

Middle Creek Publishing & Audio
9167 Pueblo Mountain Park Road
Beulah, CO 81023

editor@middlecreekpublishing.com
(719) 369-9050

First Paperback Edition, 2022
ISBN: 978-1-957483-00-9

Cover design: David Martin, using small sample of a
photograph by Allen Vogel of Townes Van Zandt's
shoulder.

"Fox" linocut print by Hannah Evans, 2022. Find more of
her work on Instagram @hannah_evans.art

Printed in the United States

Our Mother, The Mountain

Alexander Shalom Joseph

Middle Creek Publishing & Audio, LLC

Beulah, CO USA
↑

To the late poet, Dobbie Reese Norris.

You were the first person,
other than my mother,
to tell me that I was a good poet.

Thank you for being there in those early days when
a book was just a dream.

Foreword

Perhaps now it can be no other way: the poem that praises the founding of a house is also the elegy that mourns the same house's loss. The paradox only makes sense when the act of home-making mimics the making of the world entire—the domestic orders a microcosmic imitation of that grand house, the universe. So it is for Alexander Shalom Joseph, whose calendrical *Our Mother, The Mountain* takes upon itself the minute minute-to-minute attentions that makes of light itself a companion, and makes of the air a scented introduction to visitors not yet known. One of those visitors is fire, that horse galloping every summer through the West. So it is we have a small book that honors the fire we live by—the sun—and knows other fires threaten opposite ends. The conflagration. By the light of one fire, we gather together a life; by the light of another, we gather every object of care we can hold, and then we run. I suspect many readers of this volume will be sure to gather it—a little good company by which to build the next house, and the next world.

—Dan Beachy-Quick

WINTER

Home was the moment I wrote my name on the mailbox, cemented it in a five gallon bucket and put it in the ground. Home was the moment I chose the bedroom, the room with only one outside wall but still no insulation, where my body heat and the living room stove would keep me warm. And now the sky is nowhere to be seen. The ground is all white and cloudy and shapeless and glowing. I speed in darkness. Flakes fall so quickly they are no longer individual, just blurs of cold. I turn up the heat and I put on a John Prine song and I drive into the night. Home is this moment when I finally have somewhere to go.

I sit down and forget all of the profound things I had to say. The dog buries himself in a wide pile of snow and, for a second, disappears. I chew on cut wood and squint up at a blazing sky. The wind carries smoke from burnt branches and the ground is slick and see through like jewels. There are holes in my socks and in the armpit of my shirt. The yellow ware of skin makes of ring around where I sit in hot water. I let it darken over days, little pieces of me making a mark upon the white. I sleep through the night with crossed knees and long, crooked toes. The shape of the ceiling seems to shift with the light and the daytime through the square window comes in cold and outside the snow is blowing sidewise, like the weather of a tilted world.

The frost on the needles of the pines and on the crooked stalks of yellow grass makes a slow ghost of the morning. In the distance, fog clings like a stuck breath to ground that is so hard it doesn't move all. Even the birds and the wood chipper next door are muted. In the white, damp, freeze machines pass with their windows fogged and I think of all the things that have died, of all the things that are being born and all that is in between, all these branches sprayed with cold on one side but warmed and gold in the sun on the other.

There is so much to do but I do nothing. I read on the bed for hours or listen to folk records until I sleep. All the world is a mess of things and dollars but I don't bother with them. I just chop more wood for the fire and then put on a warmer pair of socks. As the light outside goes out, the glow from inside takes over, painting the pines orange, and all moves with stove flicker and pop. There is nothing but these wide mountains and me, alone in all this gentle night. The stubble of tree tips on the shadow-green mountain line like a torn edge of the earth, seeping into sky.

Day falls like something with weight and color, collecting in the basin of the valley, where the train rumbles the dusk, where the river and wind is only heard when the tracks are clear. We have left nothing untouched, even the silent sky is streaked and screaming. I stand two miles into the wilderness, the dawn breath is ice in my lungs and my exhale is a plume. I wanted to write a nature poem today, took to the trail with a notebook and a pen but across the valley I can see the lights and fractures of a mine, I can hear semis and harleys rattle the shivering birds in the dead-still pines and my tracks across the clearing seem a greedy smear.

Here is heaven, I cook brussels sprouts with balsamic and garlic cloves in my best pot, on the old white stove in a house built a century ago while the wind whips the world white and the shriek of the air across the roof is only muffled by a Van Zandt record and the sound of me humming along. Outside is harder than it's ever been but inside this black painted brick I have nine hundred square feet of my own world and in it there is so much love.

The echoes of headlights from far off plows on the two lane road down the valley, shining up towards me in tangible shafts of yellow-gold between the limbless, wind stripped pines, are the only traces of our world left amidst the snowdrifts and the bobbing treetops, but eventually they too disappear. I am left in the white wood with only my many layers of wind-proof, snow-proof, water-proof clothing, my squinted eyes, my beard and eyebrows like they are made out of ice and the dog at the end of the leash. And in the morning, when snow has made soft shapes of the hard world, I will walk around the loop again, between the buried houses, making first tracks far above the frozen dirt. On the thin air I will smell woodsmoke, brewing coffee, dryer sheets, septic fields and home. And in the distance beneath this ocean of a sky, the new sun will paint the peaks peach.

SPRING

The valley spreads apart. I drive over black dirt through low fog. There is a hole in the sky and it leaks a holy light. The smell on the air is pine and coal dust and creek water. The train tracks are rusty shadows beside the road. I think now of all the broken days, like shriveled needles on the branch of all my years. The road keeps on folding forward and turning like a bud towards the bright. Up here by the wide sky and melting mountains of March, the only free things are bluebirds, redtails, wood-peckers and me, but I am really only free when I get in my mud splattered car, put down all the windows, despite the air bite, and slam my right foot down on the gas as far as it will go.

The tickle then numb of the creek, cold like snow but flowing. I stand ankle deep, sinking in the yellow dust between the branches, and the shafts of shade and sun. Red chested birds sing and spring borne bugs fresh from the burrow, buzz and time ripples like the water through the slick rock and pebbles and the rusted out mining metal that washed down with the flood a few years back and ended up here in the woods all foreign and sharp between the roots and needles. I am standing through the hourglass, my feet wet with what's left of winter.

I want to write about bluebirds, how they
float in cobalt air like gods, or something
else so light and holy, but nothing is so
simple anymore. The cat killed a rabbit
and left it on the front steps. The mountain
view is perfect but for the cell phone
tower poking out. And last week I walked
through the woods, to the oldest tree I
know and when I came upon it, it was split
and scattered across the dirt and fractured
light fell through the clouds like rain.

I take the long way on the dirt, driving slowly through these dusty days of my hot, useless youth. Aspens bloom like green fire on the hills and today time is all over the place, today is a mix of so many years and I ride slow in the pickup, the tire spun dust spreading across the world and everything is awful, and everything is perfect. The mountains like rolling frozen titan waves of pointed green. The sun is so far away but also everywhere here catching the pollen in the air shining like gold stuck in rock and the wind is thin and cool, and when I get home, I unload wood until there is no more light and the stars poke through the sunset pink.

The melted butter light of dusk seeps onto the red needle floor of the wide woods. I carve my initials into a stump and in an hour the sky will be a quilt of splinter holes showing heaven, dots of glow which I will name and wish upon. In a year that was supposed to be the future but ended up hell, all I have is the present moment and hope, all I have is time to listen to the birdsong ringing out like soft bells as I walk back to my house in the snow and green leaves and yellow dust.

The day is wide and ends with a sky like a burning house, all red and pink and furious. The bruises on my skin shine yellow like flowers and I haven't slept well in a week. All the people I used to know are fools or maybe I am the fool but they are gone anyways and I am alone under the fire clouds as the dark comes and time keeps spinning. The day goes slowly and then all at once.

I walk barefoot, through the open kitchen door, into the curtain of hot sun and all of a sudden I can't remember winter. There is nothing cold or snowy in the whole world and the traffic on the highway roars by. The birds are building a nest on the electrical panel box and the pink tulips I thought would never grow are poking up out of the dusty ground and I can finally be outside without a coat. Yes, from the broken glass and rust and alpine dirt, the pink flowers push up and open. The birds move as if flight is not a miracle. The wind through the trees is a deep breath amidst the smell of pine needles and the glinting of fool's gold in the ground.

Low fog on a Sunday morning, on the first day in May, like driving through the sky. I swerve down the ripe green mountains into the concrete and sun, passing six blackbirds on a dying orange pine. In the walls of these canyons that bridge us to the rest of the world, the cliff faces are veined in red, white and purple flowers. Trees defy gravity to stretch out into the soft morning air to collect the dew and glint like living silver in the sun.

I stand on the grey floor, drinking coffee from a stone cup. I look down, all around my feet and across the house are grits of dirt and strands of hair; remnants of what I've done what I've carried with me until now. All these stains of yesterday left whenever I step. I sip my coffee and wonder what else I will leave behind, while outside the sky is clay and the rain washes the pollen into mustard puddles in the yard. Rain turns to puddles which evaporate into mud which dries into dirt which becomes dust which blows in my face as cars pass while I walk to the forest, on the way to where I can be quiet and alone, where every field is full of flowers showing every color I can name.

SUMMER

In these patchwork days of June and nights of raining stars, the neon of the tulips, columbine and catnip are made dull only by the sky. I sit under it all, in a yellow wind, as coal trains pass slow through the mountain and the swallows in the birdhouse I painted black, fly in and out all day. Then come the blurred hours when tree leaves and broken branches wane to splattered dots of black against the blue canvas of coming night.

I come down from the mountain behind me is the setting sun, in front of me, millions of lives and a pink and sweltering dusk, all the flicker and smog of the freeways and bars. I park my car and walk wide eyed through the ruin. For the first time in a year I see no trees, hear no birds, feel no dirt beneath my feet and my mouth tastes like ash. As soon as I can, I get back behind the wheel and retreat to the peaks where the yellow flowers grow, where I can see more stars than I can count in a decade, where at night I am completely, wonderfully, silently alone with my trees all twisted into swaying shadows, all gorgeous and jagged below the hollow moon.

Oh amber plains, below a summer fire raspberry sun, all the sky is cast in pink and gold. All the rubble of today is haloed in eerie light. I cough and swear and cry grey tears and in the pictures I take this month that nobody will ever see, I look tight muscled and rose lit like a tired old god of wood and wildflowers.

I'm making a list of what I want to save in case of that dreaded wall of flame: a gardening book, a souvenir t-shirt, a jade buddha, an empty cup; all my history spelled out in future ash. And if I flee with the sweaty clothes on my back and my five favorite books, what pieces of me like my very bones, will I lose, what will I forget to remember without all this that surrounds, what will remain in the soot and smolder if all I own is lost and all I have left is my breath. If the mountains on this smoky morning, so faint and far away, are any sign of tomorrow or how it may never come, let me go into the pink light with my windows down. Let me fade with a folk song on and a mug of coffee in my hand. If today is the last day, as the pure evil on the news makes it seem, let me glide into nothing, up and over these dusty, washboard roads.

The trees turn the July air into a blizzard of haze and heat. In a cotton-wood snow I walk to the thin river, where the water aches and bubbles and heals. There, past the highway howl, trees grow a thousand years thick and nothing seems to have moved since I've been alive, and it will stay this wild and green long after I too am gone. Meanwhile all the people pass by in their camper vans following that road straight, into the dry world beyond sight. I hear them pass, see their little clouds of dust, like kicked up ghosts that swirl and are left behind, while I take my shoes off at the front door, open the windows to let in the cool night air, and lay down on the couch to fade into the creamcicle dusk and cardinal call.

I drive towards a round mountain made phantom with fire and sun. My grandmother tells me this is a hard year. I fix her hose and get into my car. I drive towards the sea of kindling, these piles of twisted twigs and green. My father tells me he's not coming home. I drive towards a wall of smoke, twisting like a living vein of black in the air. I do not look back.

Steam rises from my body and the water thick like a spirit rising up and going out the window. In late July, I find myself alone on the mountain in the bath in the middle of the day, the window is open and through the wet air I can see wildflowers growing beside my house, purple in the amber summer light.

There's a time in the thin summer morning when all the rich and business people sleep in their quiet houses. The sun is barely a smear of heat and light in the sky and the road is empty but for work trucks and vans. It's the golden hour of working folks, all hauling to the first job, nodding as we pass, our bodies already sore and soon to be work gloved and sweating. Praise the carpenter, the roofer, the chimney sweep, the plumber: all these sacred always working fools. Scarred and hungry and limping. Each day a new hurt but the same job. Riding work trucks like crosses, making miracles then headed off to another set of messes down the road. Look behind paint, concrete drywall dust to find hard fought days, blood and years off of lives. All our little houses built on sore backs, forgotten and overlooked until we need them and they appear. Praise these saints of grease and hammer drills in carhartt rags and jeans, their workworn hands holding together this old yellow world.

Thirty seven in a thirty. I'm moving faster than anybody two hundred years ago ever did and to me it feels slow. The road is still and so is the sky, around every corner a broken down car or state patroller, radar gun in hand. I look to the pavement and see speed. I look to the trees and see so many teaching, breathing things to whom my whole little life is a blip. And the forests will burn and all roads will empty and the cities will turn to rubble and from pine ash will grow aspen fields and the birdsong will ring, uninhibited. And now I follow a red truck through a dead valley, sure there is still green here, but soon in the sun all will wilt and wane to straw, dust and kindling. On the horizon past the yellow hills, a storm collects like a wide ghost of long-gone mountains and if it rains the highway will turn to mud.

I wake in tangerine light, read the news and fear all this is dying. Way north, beyond the border they are cutting down the biggest trees in the world, leaving stumps like headstones of the forest, so large ten bodies fit it one and down here in the high, yellow desert our houses swim in trees, but soon they or the fires will come to make another graveyard where these great woodlands once swayed in the pollen breeze. I step outside into the gold glint of the dirt and already spinning heat and traffic sound, the mockingbirds make a song of the air and the day is crisp and piney. I think it is just us who build the cities and roads, it is just us who broke the cycle. I think that those who float in water and sky will find a way with or without all that we break and bury and buy, I hope that without us they will find a way.

In the end remember, after the fires rush
like starved horses through the trees, after
the well is useless and rusted, after the sky
is smoke, after these roads and rivers are
ruin, after these bricks are blacker than
ever, and the roof is raw charcoal and
dust, in the end remember while we could
we laughed in the woods, walked past
wind whipped branches, bought cheap
lottery tickets and lost, drank the local gin
from wide glasses, saw more stars nightly
than most ever do, in the end remember
while we could, we took the slow roads,
made Saturdays last for so long, made the
windows foggy, snuck to the mountain
top to see it all, made the most of every
moment we could, in the end, when all is
what we feared it would be, remember all
that will waste wasn't wasted by us.

I used to fear the fire, the ember storm, like so many hearts of pure heat, the black sky, the ground turned sterile forever, but last week as I sweat hauling slash and charred trunks where five years before a great wave of flame consumed everything in sight, there was now knee high grass and purple flowers and there was life, so much green and color where once there was only soot and the fear waned to surrender and there was something sweet like the butterscotch of pine sap on the wind.

An hour past the dawn and the light is still cherry wine. The birds are asong like a chorus hidden in the trees. The wind is thin and hinted with distant smoke. The cars are not yet out, neither are the planes, for the sky is bluer than water and the heat of the day is a mere whisper of noon. The paintbrush and the columbine open in the sweet light and the day reeks of color and sugar. I walk to the stream and there I find water like watch glass, so clean and clear I can forget it's even there. Time tumbles between river rocks: things being born, things dying as the day turns hot then gold and then the sun is replaced by its nighttime ghost, which hangs so swollen and pearly over all these sleeping trees.

I too know the red wheelbarrow in the rain, how the colors pop and shine as the water falls. How in the weather the air is thick and alive. How there is no sound but the droplets on the roof, a symphony of tiny hammers all playing at once, as the barrow fills with water and tips over into the overgrown technicolor grass. And when some plants are dying, they bloom like never before. A finale of living fragrant color; a mountain stained all red and yellow and pink. And I don't know what will live or what will die or what is dead already, but I am loving the flowers and I walk through them in a thin rain that carries with it the cold of the coming months.

FALL

Now I've lived here long enough that all the mail in the box has my name on it and no others, none of the decades of renters or other passersby and I guess that makes it home. This little black brick haven tucked in the heart of the woods where I see Orion through the window as I fall asleep and where the wind whistles so many sweet songs. Here the season is told by the wind in tall grasses. The season is told by how the whole valley moves like blonde and rippled hair, by the way the light is all honey and rose through the branches and streams and old yellowed windows which show the world in sepia squares. The season is told by the way the light wanes, how the darkness takes more of every day, how we move inside like bears ready to sleep the winter away.

The warmth of the night, beneath patterned blankets, drips away as I walk through the forest at dawn with the dog in tow. The grass stands up straight in the frigid fresh air, straight like it too feels a chill. There is no wind. There are no passing cars. Here the myth of silence is made real in the soundless flight of a jay across the meadow. The aspen leaves like honey and embers and liquid gold. The air of the day is hot, the nights all frigid and fogged and make me pull that extra blanket up from under the bed. The sunsets are violent with color, just splintering the evening into neon and peach, stopping cars in the road with gape jawed drivers. It feels like winter and summer all at once and the peaks bare as the moon, long for snow.

I walk on white yellow ground swirled in new snow and clumped dead dirt. The open valley is loud with car sounds and daylight. Eventually I come upon a herd of cattle, their brown and black shocked and highlighted against the snow. They sit and snort and cast jets of steam from their ringed noses, steam which swirls into the day. They pay me no mind but for a slight turn of theirs heads and horns. I pass through them and up towards a peak, which looks out into white. The wind makes moans of the mountain and the trees rock in double, triple time, the movement of the air and ice is music in that it deafens the loud of the world and I am left in the thatch of pine, post holing through knee high drift sinking in that sacred silence of earthly noise.

Two days after moving into my place on the mountain, it came across the yard like a living flame. So weightless on its paws it could have been floating, its tail the definition of orange all bushy and black edged, this being, this seemingly sacred thing, my first neighbor to welcome me home. Then a month after that, it was sitting in my driveway this small beast of fall colors and watching eyes, its den somewhere close, licking its paws like a pet. And in the last year, I smile when I see it. Sometimes it is just a flash in the corner of my vision, sometimes we stare at each other, me chopping wood or working on my fence. It is my friend this fox, it has become something I long to see. But tonight on the way home, on the last curve before the top, there in the other lane it lay unmoving, it's mouth half open, its eyes squinted shut. My friend in the road, hit and left. Another lovely thing torn away by us, us who stain the sky with false light and noise. Us who kill and cut and ruin. And I am a part of it all and my neighbor is dead in the road. I wish I could blame a tourist or a drunk driving carelessly, but it could have been me. It was me. It was us. It was all of us. What have we done? What have we done, my friend.

Light through bare trunked trees, snow in
that light swirling and gold. I see this
through the kitchen window as coffee
steam rises, while the day is young and
cold still. I think about how there is so
much to know and do that I will never get
to, but I find ease and home in this place
in these mountains and how the wind
whistles as it moves the sky.

Rivers low this time of year. Grey rocks wind down the valleys and the cars in the pink dusk, puff out smoke like breath. The hills are embers, all the colors of fire held loosely by the trees, sounding like applause in the fogged breeze.

Acknowledgements

I would especially like to thank:

My parents, my sister, my grandmother and the rest of my family for urging me on and for always answering another one of my rambling calls.

Barb Hardt and Sara Sandstrom for believing in my poetry enough to put it in their newspaper, The Mountain Ear, every week for the last two years.

Townes Van Zandt, Phil Elverum, Colter Wall, Kora Feder, Tyler Childers and Adrienne Lenker: your music is the soundtrack to this book and to my best days.

My friends, muses and collaborators: Bradford, Robin, Josey, Chris, Madeline, Charlie and everyone else.

My mentors, for without my guides I am lost: Jeffery Duvall, Chris Rosales, Sean Murphy, Eric Darton, Rachel Weaver, Hoag Holmgren, Mike Parker, Michelle NakaPierce,, Dan Beachy-Quick, J'Lyn Chapman, Philip Levine, Charles Bukowski, David Foster Wallace and Cormac McCarthy.

And finally, to David Anthony Martin. Back in my days as a chimney sweep on these mountain rooves, I would imagine, as I balanced on ladders in the ripping wind, that one day you would accept one of my poetry books for publication. Our Mother, the Mountain was written for you to publish, I submitted it only to you and am so honored by your excitement about and commitment to this book.

About the Author

It's said in the Talmud that there are three ways to be a good Jew: study, prayer and acts of loving kindness — Alexander Shalom Joseph thinks of his writing and work as a teacher as a mix of all three. Alexander is the author of three published books and many published individual poems and short stories. His published books include the story collection *American Wasteland*, published by Owl Canyon Press, the novella. *The Last of the Light*, published by Orison Books and the poetry collection *Our Mother the Mountain*, published by Middle Creek Publishing. His Novels and Short Stories have been short listed/ finalists/ or semi-finalists for many literary prizes. Alexander has an MFA from The Jack Kerouac School, and an MA in English Education and lives in a cabin in rural Colorado.

About Middle Creek Publishing

MIDDLE CREEK PUBLISHING strongly believes that responding to the world through art & literature — and sharing that response — is a vital part of being an artist.

MIDDLE CREEK PUBLISHING is a company seeking to make the world a better place through both the means and ends of publishing. We are publishers of quality literature in any genre from authors and artists, both seasoned and as-yet undervalued, with a great interest in works which may be considered to be, illuminate or embody any aspect of contemplative Human Ecology, defined as the relationship between humans and their natural, social, and built environments.

MIDDLE CREEK PUBLISHING's particular interest in Human Ecology, is meant to clarify an aspect of the quality in the works we will consider for publication, and is meant as a guide to those considering submitting work to us. Our interest is in publishing works illuminating the Human experience through words, story or other content that connects us to each other, our environment, our history and our potential deeply and more consciously.

Made in the USA
Monee, IL
20 July 2023